Pacific Explorers

Phillip Simpson

Pacific Explorers

Text: Phillip Simpson
Publishers: Tania Mazzeo and Eliza Webb
Series consultant: Amanda Sutera
Hands on Heads Consulting
Editor: Sarah Layton
Project editor: Annabel Smith
Designer: Leigh Ashforth
Project designer: Danielle Maccarone
Illustrations: Zak Waipara
Maps: Wayne Murphy
Permissions researcher: Lumina Datamatics
Production controller: Renee Tome

Acknowledgements
We would like to thank the following for permission to reproduce copyright material:

Back cover p. 1, p. 8: iStock.com/ilbusca; p. 6 (top): Nature Picture Library/Alamy Stock Photo, (bottom): Manfred Thürig/Alamy Stock Photo; p. 9 (top left): David Wall/Alamy Stock Photo, (top right): Fernand-P/Shutterstock.com, (bottom): Eric PINEL/Alamy Stock Photo; p. 32, p. 10 (top): EMU history/Alamy Stock Photo, (bottom): IanDagnall Computing/Alamy Stock Photo; p. 1, p. 11: Digital Vision./Photodisc/Getty Images; p. 12: Westend61 GmbH/Alamy Stock Photo; p. 13: Matteo Colombo/Moment/Getty Images; p. 16: © Anders Ryma; p. 17: Genevieve Vallee/Alamy Stock Photo; p. 18: Niday Picture Library/Alamy Stock Photo; p. 19 (top): Panoramic Images/Alamy Stock Photo, (bottom): Maximilian Laschon/Alamy Stock Vector; p. 20: Maridav/Alamy Stock Photo; p. 22: iStock.com/Claudio Pepe; p. 24: iStock.com/Candyfloss-Film; p. 25 (top): Imogen Warren/Shutterstock.com, (bottom): Gabrielle/Adobe Stock Photos; p. 26: Pictorial Press Ltd/Alamy Stock Photo; p. 27 (top): Karel Lorier/Alamy Stock Photo, (bottom:; dpa picture alliance/Alamy Stock Photo.

Every effort has been made to trace and acknowledge copyright. However, if any infringement has occurred, the publishers tender their apologies and invite the copyright holders to contact them.

NovaStar

ISBN 978 0 17 033475 4

Cengage Learning Australia
Level 5, 80 Dorcas Street
Southbank VIC 3006 Australia
Phone: 1300 790 853
Email: aust.nelsonprimary@cengage.com

For learning solutions, visit **cengage.com.au**

Printed in Malaysia by Papercraft
1 2 3 4 5 6 7 29 28 27 26 25

Nelson acknowledges the Traditional Owners and Custodians of the lands of all First Nations Peoples. We pay respect to Elders past and present, and extend that respect to all First Nations Peoples today.

Contents

Guided by Nature

Have you ever thought about how you would find your way somewhere without a map or phone? What if you were in a place with very few **landmarks**, like the middle of the ocean? And what if it was dark?

Over 3000 years ago, Pacific explorers found ways to overcome these and other challenges so they could travel from place to place.

Pacific explorers travelled across the ocean thousands of years ago.

The Pacific Ocean

The Pacific Ocean is the largest ocean on Earth. It covers about one-third of Earth's surface. It is so big that it stretches from the Arctic Ocean in the north down to the edge of the Southern Ocean around Antarctica. It touches the shores of many continents, including Australia, Asia, and North and South America.

The Pacific Ocean has different **currents**. Currents are like rivers of water flowing through the ocean in certain directions. They can be warm or cold, and they affect the weather. They can also affect how easy or hard it is to sail on the ocean.

Pacific Ocean Currents

The North and South Pacific currents are created by circular wind patterns.

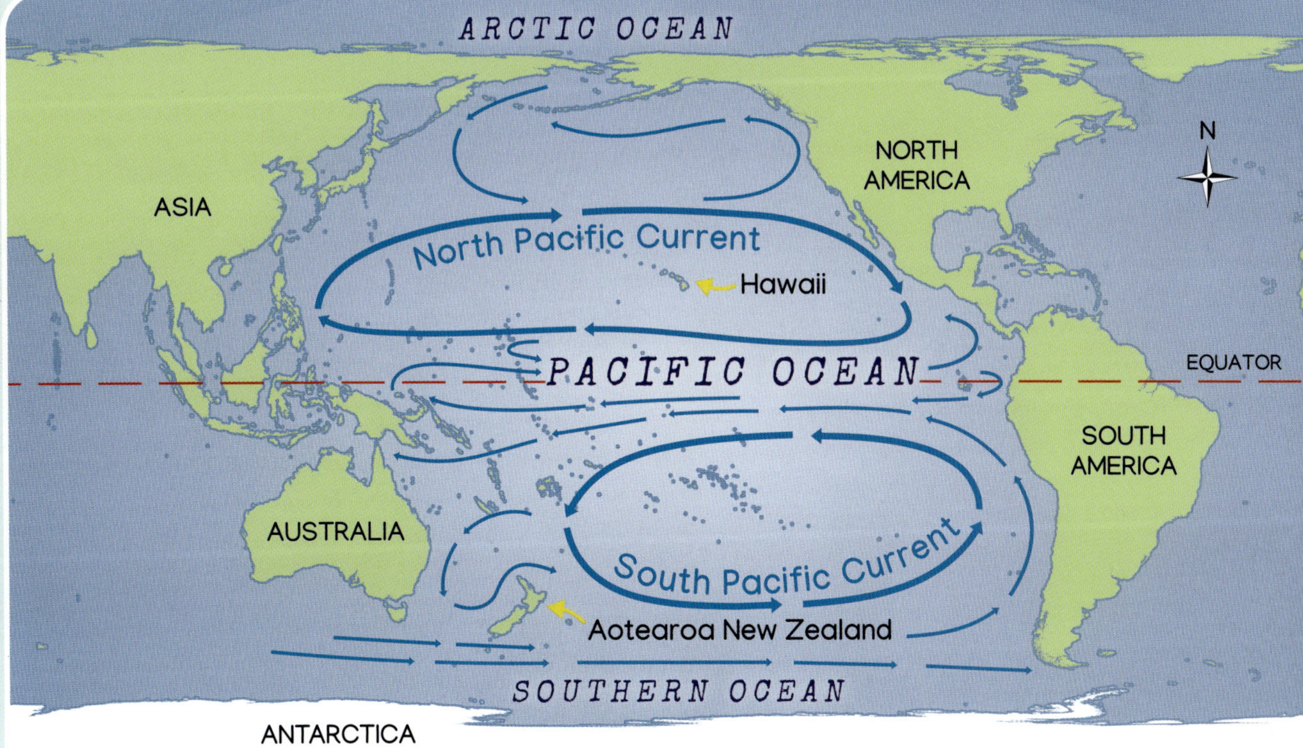

Because it covers so much of Earth, the Pacific Ocean has a wide range of weather patterns. Near the equator, the water is warm, and the weather is often sunny. This part of the Pacific Ocean has coral reefs and brightly coloured fish. But further south, the water is very cold – the perfect habitat for animals like penguins and seals.

A green turtle swims in warmer Pacific ocean water near the equator.

A colony of rockhopper penguins live in the southern Pacific Ocean, close to the cold waters around Antarctica.

Polynesia

In the central and south Pacific Ocean, there is a huge **region** made up of more than 1000 islands, called Polynesia. Some well-known places in Polynesia are Aotearoa New Zealand, Samoa, Hawaii and Tahiti.

The Māori People

The Polynesian islands were the last places on Earth to be settled. Aotearoa New Zealand was the final place, with Polynesian peoples arriving sometime between 1200 and 1300 **CE**. These settlers were the **ancestors** of the Māori people.

A Map of Polynesia

Polynesia is a large area in the central and south Pacific Ocean made up of many islands.

Polynesian people were very skilled sailors and explorers. They developed **effective** methods of finding their way around the ocean, using nature.

Polynesian people invented new kinds of boats, which they used to discover and **settle** new islands and spread Polynesian languages, traditions and ways of life across huge distances.

Sailing the Pacific

Polynesian people started to explore the Pacific islands around 3000 years ago. There are many possible reasons for their explorations – from finding new land to just being curious about unknown areas of the world. The journey between Polynesian islands needed skilled **navigators**, courage and, of course, suitable boats.

Canoes

Polynesian explorers sailed around the Pacific Ocean in large canoes, which are lightweight boats with narrow **hulls**. They made different types of canoes: some had just one hull, some were double-hulled and some were outrigger canoes. Outrigger canoes have one large hull and another smaller hull attached to one side for balance.

The design of outrigger canoes hasn't changed in many centuries.

Single-hulled canoes were often used for short trips. Double-hulled and outrigger canoes were more stable, so they were used for longer journeys and in rough waters. They could sail very fast and carry up to 80 people.

This single-hulled Māori canoe (a *waka*) is launched each year to celebrate Waitangi Day in Aotearoa New Zealand.

A traditional double-hulled canoe is displayed in Tahiti, French Polynesia.

Some of the Polynesian islands are more than 1000 kilometres apart. To sail such a distance in a canoe would take five or six weeks.

People from different parts of Polynesia designed and built different types of canoes, but all of them used materials found locally, like wood and strong plant **fibres**. Skilled craftspeople carefully carved the wood to create the hulls. They used the fibres to make ropes to tie all the materials together.

Good Design

The basic design of outrigger canoes is still used around the world today. Catamarans (a type of boat with two hulls) and trimarans (a boat with three hulls) are based on outrigger canoes and are used in sailing races.

a catamaran

Sails and Paddles

Many canoes had big sails made from **woven** leaves or mats. The sails caught the wind, helping the canoes to move faster and giving the sailors a rest from paddling.

Explorers from different parts of Polynesia developed many different sail shapes and sizes to work best in the winds they experienced more often.

This illustration of a canoe from Hawaii (1779) shows its triangular woven sail.

The Need for Speed

The British explorer Captain James Cook (one of the first Europeans to arrive in the Pacific region) noticed that a Polynesian canoe, called a *pahi*, could sail faster than his ship, the *Endeavour*. Cook wrote in his journal that a pahi "may with ease sail 40 leagues (around 200 kilometres) a day or more".

Captain James Cook

With their specially designed canoes, the Polynesian explorers were ready to travel across the Pacific Ocean, find new lands and settle in different places. But how did they know which way to go, and how to find their way back again?

Finding the Way

The people who helped Polynesian explorers travel across the Pacific Ocean were sometimes called "wayfinders". Wayfinders used their knowledge of the seas, stars, clouds, winds and animals to **navigate** the Pacific Ocean. They used nature's signs to work out which direction to travel across huge distances.

Polynesian explorers sailed as far north as Hawaii and all the way south to Rapa Nui (Easter Island) and Aotearoa New Zealand. Crossing such enormous distances was dangerous, but wayfinders were very skilled navigators. They used their deep understanding of nature's signs, like the movement of the stars and the direction of ocean currents, to safely guide their canoes through previously unexplored waters.

Polynesian Exploration

After arriving from Asia, Polynesian explorers settled many Pacific islands over the next 2000 years.

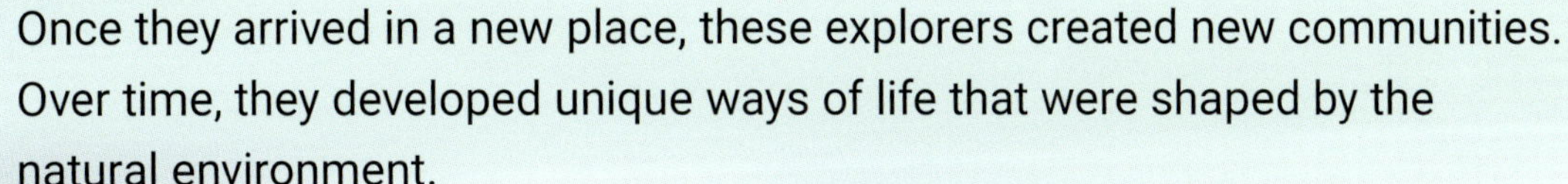

Once they arrived in a new place, these explorers created new communities. Over time, they developed unique ways of life that were shaped by the natural environment.

Outrigger canoes are still used today for leisure activities and tourism.

Special Knowledge

Knowledge of how to navigate the Pacific Ocean was often kept secret by wayfinders and only shared among families or within special **guilds**. Members of the navigator guilds were very well respected. They were important leaders in their communities.

Wayfinding knowledge was valuable because it allowed Pacific explorers to discover new islands, with new sources of food and land to settle. They could visit and trade with neighbouring communities.

Polynesian peoples had no alphabet or way of writing, so their special knowledge was passed down orally. This meant the older **generations** shared information with the younger members of the community through stories, songs, chants, conversations and *karakia* (Māori prayers).

Secret Skills

The knowledge of how to build canoes that could travel long distances was kept a secret within the navigator guilds.

An experienced wayfinder teaches young men wayfinding techniques in a *maneaba* (a meeting house).

Learning from Others

A wayfinder's education started at a young age. Experienced wayfinders taught their **apprentices** how to "read" the Sun, clouds, waves and stars, and to observe certain marine animals to help them find their way.

Young apprentices went on sea voyages with skilled wayfinders for hands-on learning. Some experienced wayfinders would place stones, shells and sticks in the sand or on mats to make a "star compass", which helped them to navigate using the stars. They also made "stick charts" of the ocean's winds, waves and currents.

Master wayfinder Mau Piailug (centre) teaches his son and grandson how to use a star compass.

Guided by Memory

Every wayfinder had their own method for making a stick chart, so often the chart could only be read by that navigator or someone they had taught. The wayfinder memorised the chart before a voyage and then relied on their memory to guide the canoe .

A stick chart is displayed at the Te Ara Museum of Cultural Enterprise in Rarotonga, Cook Islands.

Using Nature to Navigate

Before European explorers arrived in Polynesia bringing tools like **magnetic compasses**, printed maps and ocean charts, Pacific wayfinders had their own ways of navigating the vast ocean. European navigators used the Sun and the stars to navigate across oceans, too, but their information was written down. Pacific wayfinders kept all their knowledge in their memories!

European explorers journeying to Polynesia would have been used to maps like this one of Europe from 1740.

Chasing the Sun

The most basic way to tell direction at sea is to look at the Sun. The Sun was the main guide for Pacific wayfinders because they could observe exactly where it rose and set, and where it was in the sky during the day. They knew that if they followed the Sun, they would travel west.

The Sun sets in the west over the Pacific Ocean.

The Speed of Light

Most Polynesian people believed in a Sun god, often called Rā. Māori people believed that, in the past, the Sun used to move too quickly across the sky. Then, a demigod (half-human, half-god) called Māui made the Sun slow down, giving people more light during the day.

the Polynesian Sun god, Rā (or Tama-nui-te-rā)

Watching the Clouds

Wayfinders paid close attention to the shape and movement of clouds. Certain cloud shapes meant land was nearby, and others suggested that the weather was about to change.

Low-lying islands and coral reefs cannot be seen from far away, and they can cause a lot of damage to a canoe. Pacific wayfinders looked at the bottoms of clouds to check for a **reflection** of the lighter, shallow water usually found around an island or reef, and quickly steered the canoe away.

Some cloud shapes and colours told navigators when a big storm was coming, helping them to change direction in time.

The light-coloured sands of the beach and the dark blue of the ocean are reflected on the bottoms of clouds off the shore of Fakarava Atoll, French Polynesia.

Moving With the Waves and Currents

If there were no clouds in sight, a wayfinder could use other natural signs to navigate the ocean. Wayfinders were also known to use ocean wave patterns as a guide.

Pacific wayfinders knew that islands disrupt waves by bouncing them back or changing their direction. An experienced navigator could see and feel the change in the wave pattern and know the canoe was near an island, even though they couldn't see the island yet.

Curving Waves

Waves change direction when they get close to land, curving to flow towards it.

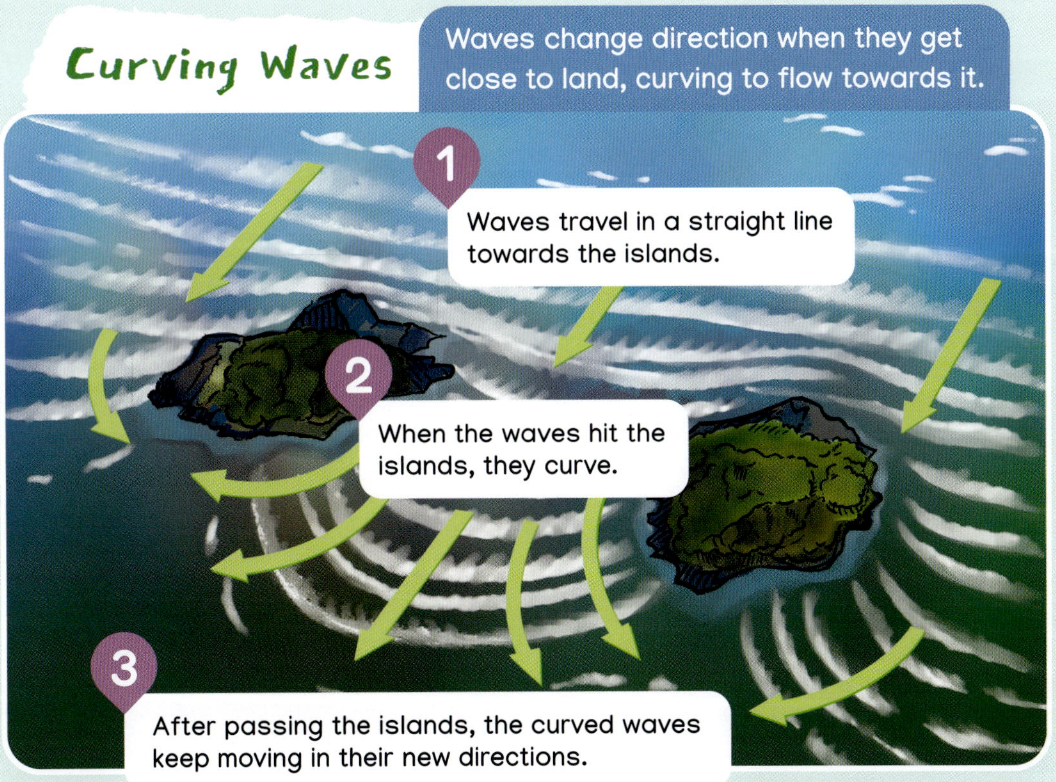

Pacific navigators also understood the currents in different parts of the ocean. They could look at the surface of the water and know which direction it would take the canoe.

Tracking the Stars

Once the Sun had set, steering a canoe by tracking the stars was the most accurate way to navigate the ocean. Wayfinders were experts at reading the stars in the night sky. They knew that stars always rise in the east and set in the west, and that different stars can be seen at different times of the year and in different locations.

The best navigators could memorise the rising and setting positions of hundreds of stars. They also knew that these stars would rise earlier or later each night as the seasons changed.

Constellations fill the sky over the island of Bora Bora, French Polynesia.

Pacific wayfinders could find their way around an ocean even when they couldn't see any land, and they always knew how to get home by remembering which stars would be near a particular island at a certain time of year.

Star paths, like all wayfinder knowledge, had to be taught and memorised.

Sailing with the Stars

European explorers needed tools like compasses and maps to guide them. In contrast, wayfinders needed to identify just 10 to 12 stars in the sky – a "star path" – to accurately steer their canoe.

Observing Bioluminescence

Some living things can glow in the dark. This is called "bioluminescence". Certain kinds of **plankton** glow as they drift near the surface of the ocean, creating flashing lights in the waves. Pacific wayfinders used the plankton's bioluminescence to see the ocean currents and waves at night – the flashing lights got faster the closer the plankton were to land. This told the navigator how far it was to the nearest island.

Plankton's bioluminescence is sometimes called "the sea sparkle".

Experiments with Wayfinding

Modern-day scientists have tested wayfinding skills by sailing traditional canoes around the Pacific Ocean using only Polynesian wayfinding tools and methods of navigation. With no compasses, maps or **GPS**, they successfully found their way around vast sections of **open ocean**.

Following the Birds

Birds were also an important natural sign for Pacific wayfinders. Polynesian navigators watched the flight patterns of flocks of birds for clues about the location of islands in the ocean. Some kinds of birds could only fly short distances, so if a navigator spotted that bird in the sky, it meant land was nearby.

Shining cuckoos might have helped Polynesian explorers discover Aotearoa New Zealand, because the cuckoos migrate there every year in spring.

Frigatebirds will usually stay close to land, helping wayfinders to know land was nearby.

Keeping the Knowledge Alive

Polynesian wayfinders used their strong relationship with nature to explore and settle islands across the Pacific Ocean, long before European explorers arrived. Wayfinders used the Sun and stars, clouds, currents and creatures to guide them. And with no writing system, they had to memorise it all!

Sadly, because these skills were mainly shared orally, some knowledge has been lost over time. Sailing the ocean was dangerous, and sometimes wayfinders were lost at sea before they had shared their knowledge.

When European explorers came to Polynesia, they brought new navigation techniques and modern tools, so Polynesian wayfinding knowledge started to disappear.

A European man speaks with Tahitian people aboard a ceremonial canoe, 1820.

Magnets and Myths

European explorers reached Polynesia in the late nineteenth century, using their scientific navigation tools like printed maps and magnetic compasses. These modern explorers couldn't believe that Polynesian people had found, and moved around, different Pacific islands using just nature's signs. They assumed the Polynesians had discovered new islands by accident. Although this was untrue, it became a common **myth**.

People learn about traditional canoes from a Māori elder on Waitangi Day.

The different Polynesian communities have been shaped by their relationship with nature, particularly the ocean. Today, they are saving and celebrating their wayfinding knowledge by recording it and continuing to practise it.

Māori men race *waka* canoes in Aotearoa New Zealand in 2015.

The Legend of Kupe and the Giant Octopus

Retold by
Phillip Simpson

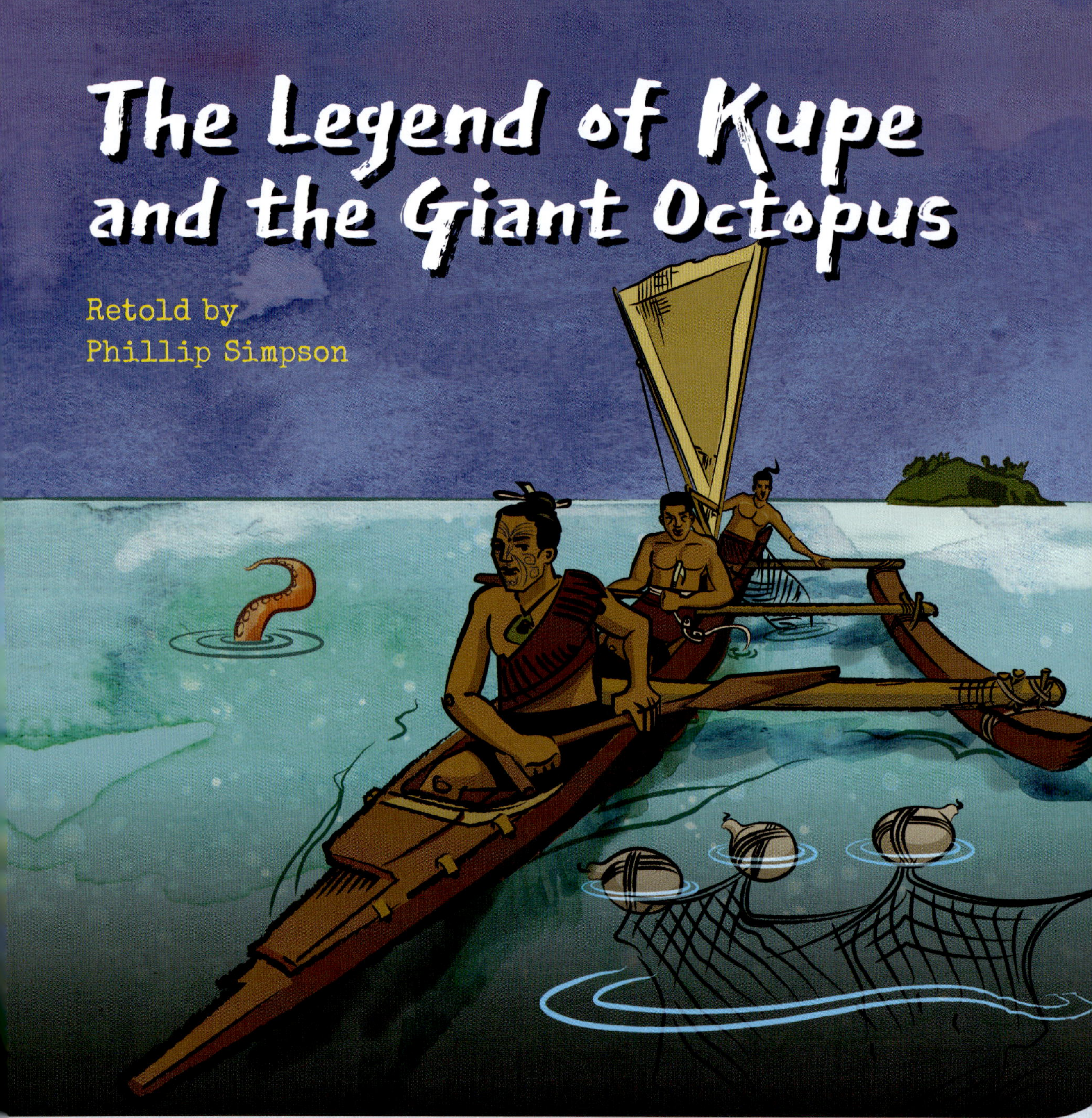

Long ago, a brave fisherman and respected leader named Kupe (pronounced *koo-pay*) lived in a place called Hawaiki.

One day, something strange happened to Kupe and his crew of fishermen. Usually, when they tossed their fishing hooks into the water, a hungry fish would take the bait and the fishermen would catch it. However, on this day, the bait was gone – but the fishermen caught no fish.

Kupe suspected that a giant octopus was causing all the trouble. The octopus belonged to Muturangi, an important **elder** in the community. Kupe discovered that the sneaky octopus was taking the fishermen's bait.

Kupe went to talk to Muturangi and asked him to control his pet octopus. But Muturangi refused, saying the octopus wasn't to blame. He accused the fishermen of disrespecting the gods of the sea and said that was why they had caught no fish.

The octopus kept stealing their fish, so Kupe got ready for a battle. He and his crew – including his wife, Hine-te-aparangi (pronounced *hin-eh tee-apa-rang-ee*) – sailed a strong canoe out to sea. They chased the giant octopus for weeks over a great distance. Kupe was an experienced wayfinder. During the voyage, he observed the positions of the stars so he could find his way home.

Eventually, far ahead, the crew saw some land with a long, white cloud over it. It was a land they had never seen before. Hine-te-aparangi named the land Aotearoa (now also called New Zealand), or the "long white cloud".

After exploring the new land, Kupe and his crew continued to chase the giant octopus, and Kupe eventually killed it. It was a great victory, but Kupe's real prize was this beautiful new land of the long white cloud.

Author Note

Hawaiki was the homeland of the Māori people. No one knows exactly where it was, but it was most likely in the eastern islands of Polynesia, possibly the Society Islands, the southern Cook Islands and the Austral Islands in French Polynesia.

Glossary

ancestors (*noun*)	family members who lived a long time ago
apprentices (*noun*)	people who learn from another person with more knowledge, usually how to do a job
CE (*noun*)	years since the beginning of the Common Era
currents (*noun*)	strong and quick movements of water
effective (*adjective*)	successful or working well
elder (*noun*)	a person of experience and authority, usually older
fibres (*noun*)	small, thin threads that make up materials such as wool or cotton
generations (*noun*)	all the people born and living at around the same time
GPS (*noun*)	Global Positioning System: a navigation system that allows users to determine their exact location
guilds (*noun*)	groups of people who do the same job or who have the same interests
hulls (*noun*)	the main parts or body of a ship
landmarks (*noun*)	visible things in your surroundings that help you know where you are
magnetic compasses (*noun*)	tools using a magnet that points to the north
myth (*noun*)	a story that many people believe, but that is not true
navigate (*verb*)	to plan a path from one place to another
navigators (*noun*)	people who plan the course of a ship
open ocean (*noun*)	part of the ocean where no land can be seen
plankton (*noun*)	very tiny living creatures found in water
reflection (*noun*)	an image in a mirror, on a shiny surface or on water
region (*noun*)	a large area of land that usually doesn't have exact borders
settle (*verb*)	to make a place your home forever
woven (*adjective*)	made by crossing pieces of material or threads over and under in a pattern

Index